How Should I Think about Money?

Crucial Questions booklets provide a quick introduction to definitive Christian truths. This expanding collection includes titles such as:

Who Is Jesus?

Can I Trust the Bible?

Does Prayer Change Things?

Can I Know God's Will?

How Should I Live in This World?

What Does It Mean to Be Born Again?

Can I Be Sure I'm Saved?

What Is Faith?

What Can I Do with My Guilt?

What Is the Trinity?

TO BROWSE THE REST OF THE SERIES,
PLEASE VISIT: **REFORMATIONTRUST.COM/CQ**

CQ

How Should I Think about Money?

R.C. SPROUL

ℍℝ *Reformation Trust*   A DIVISION OF LIGONIER MINISTRIES, ORLANDO, FL

How Should I Think about Money?
© 2016 by R.C. Sproul

Published by Reformation Trust Publishing
A division of Ligonier Ministries
421 Ligonier Court, Sanford, FL 32771
Ligonier.org   ReformationTrust.com

Printed in China
RR Donnelley
0001018
First edition, third printing

ISBN 978-1-64289-058-7 (Paperback)
ISBN 978-1-64289-086-0 (ePub)
ISBN 978-1-64289-114-0 (Kindle)

Cover design: Ligonier Creative
Interior typeset: Katherine Lloyd, The DESK

All Scripture quotations are from the ESV® Bible (The Holy Bible, English Standard Version®), copyright © 2001 by Crossway, a publishing ministry of Good News Publishers. Used by permission. All rights reserved.

Library of Congress Cataloging-in-Publication Data

Sproul, R.C. (Robert Charles), 1939-2017 author.
Title: How should I think about money? / by R.C. Sproul.
Description: Orlando, FL : Reformation Trust Publishing, 2016. | Series:
  Crucial questions series ; No. 23
Identifiers: LCCN 2016011431 | ISBN 9781567695076
Subjects: LCSH: Christian stewardship. | Money--Religious aspects--
Christianity. | Economics--Religious aspects--Christianity. | Wealth--
Religious aspects--Christianity.
Classification: LCC BV772 .S69 2016 | DDC 241/.68--dc23
LC record available at https://lccn.loc.gov/201601143

Contents

Chapter One

Taking Care of Our House

We all appreciate words of commendation from those we serve—our coaches, bosses, or others in positions of authority. This desire for commendation reaches its apex when it comes to our greatest authority, our Lord and King, Jesus Christ. A word of commendation from Christ is the ultimate commendation for our servanthood. Every Christian longs to hear a certain phrase at the end of his life, words that will come from the mouth of Christ: "Well done, good and faithful servant."

The concept in the New Testament that describes and defines what it means to be a servant before Christ is the word *stewardship*. In these pages, we will explore this idea. There is a link between the biblical concept of stewardship and the academic discipline of economics, which will also be addressed.

Economics and the ethical and emotional issues that surround it are frequent topics of discussion and front-page news items. This is particularly true in an election year, when much of the debate focuses on economic issues. What we don't see initially is that other issues, such as education and abortion, are also questions of economics. Broadly understood, economics has to do not only with money or taxes or business but with the management of resources. That includes all of our resources, such as the resource of our unborn children and educational materials and policies.

In other words, how we use our resources is the subject of economics, and in a biblical sense it is the chief concern of stewardship. Consider the verbal link between stewardship and economics. The English word *economics* and *economy* come from the Greek word *oikonomia,* which is made up of two parts: *oikos,* the word for "house" or "household," and *nomos,* the word for "law." So, *oikos* and *nomos* together literally mean "house law."

Oikonomia is transliterated into English as "economy." The English word that translates—rather than transliterates—the word *oikonomia* is the English word *stewardship*. So, stewardship and economics are closely related concepts, and in fact, to a New Testament Christian, there was no distinction between them.

A steward in the ancient world was a person who was given the responsibility and authority to rule over the affairs of the household. For example, the patriarch Joseph became a steward over Potiphar's household: he managed everything in the household and was given the authority to rule over the house (Gen. 39:1–6a). In that role, he was responsible to manage the household well; he was not to waste the resources of the family but to make wise decisions.

Yet, the role of the steward was not something that just happened to emerge in the Greek system of management, nor was it something invented by the Egyptians in the time of Joseph. The steward's role derives from the principle of stewardship, which is rooted in the creation of mankind.

Look at the foundations for stewardship found in the early chapters of Genesis. In Genesis 1:26–28, we read:

Then God said, "Let us make man in our image, after our likeness. And let them have dominion over the fish of the sea and over the birds of the heavens and over the livestock and over all the earth and over every creeping thing that creeps on the earth." So God created man in his own image, in the image of God he created him; male and female he created them. And God blessed them. And God said to them, "Be fruitful and multiply and fill the earth and subdue it, and have dominion over the fish of the sea and over the birds of the heavens and over every living thing that moves on the earth."

On the very first page of the Bible, we see the creation of human beings—made in the image of God, who revealed Himself initially as the Creator of all things—and the subsequent call of His image bearers to imitate Him in a certain way: by being productive. Human beings were commanded to be fruitful and multiply. This was a command for productivity, which has stewardship implications. Thus, the concern for stewardship is rooted in creation.

Sometimes we think that the New Testament is not concerned with labor, industry, or productivity, but it is concerned only that we love each other and live by grace and not by works. But if we examine the parables and language of Jesus, we see an emphasis on the call to fruitfulness. Jesus calls His people to be fruitful not only in the multiplication of the species through propagation, but for the kingdom's sake. This is an expansion of the creation ordinance that His people are to be productive.

The second command given to Adam and Eve was to have dominion over the earth. God installed Adam and Eve as His vice-regents, those who were to rule in His stead over all of creation. It's not that God granted independent ownership of the planet to humankind. It remains His possession. But God called Adam and Eve to exercise authority over the animals, plants, seas, rivers, sky, and the environment. They were not to exercise authority like a reckless tyrant who has carte blanche to do anything he wants, for God didn't make Adam and Eve owners of the earth. He made them stewards of the earth, who were to act in His name and for His glory.

Immediately after giving this mandate, God created a lush and gorgeous garden and placed Adam and Eve in it (Gen. 2:15). He commanded them "to work it and keep it." This command to work and keep is key to understanding the responsibility that is given to human beings, which goes with the privileged status of being made in God's image and being given dominion over the earth.

At creation, the mandate that God gave to humanity was for people to reflect and mirror God's stewardship over this sphere of creation. This involves far more than religious enterprises or the church. It has to do with how we engage in scientific endeavors, how we do business, how we treat each other, how we treat animals, and how we treat the environment. That dominion over the earth is not a license to exploit, pillage, consume, or destroy the earth; it is a responsibility to exercise stewardship over our home by working and keeping it. Working and keeping one's home means preventing it from falling apart, keeping it orderly, maintaining it, preserving it, and making it beautiful. The whole science of ecology is rooted and grounded in this principle. God didn't say, "From now on, all of your food will fall to you out of heaven." He said, "You are to work with Me in being productive: dressing, tilling, planting, replenishing, and so on."

The next commandment that was given to Adam and Eve in the garden was to name the animals (Gen. 2:19). In its most elementary sense, this was the birth of science:

learning to distinguish among species, kinds, and forms, and discerning reality as we examine it. This is also part of our stewardship—learning about the place where we live and caring about it. These principles are not simply for one's own house but for the entire planet.

Some are old enough to remember the astonishing achievement of twentieth-century Americans when the first astronauts were sent to the moon. Inevitably, part of that memory includes astronaut Neil Armstrong's first footsteps on the moon and when he spoke of a giant step for mankind. One could look at that human achievement simply in terms of human arrogance—or we could see it as a fulfillment of the mandate that God gave us to have dominion over creation.

Fundamentally, stewardship is about exercising our God-given dominion over His creation, reflecting the image of our creator God in His care, responsibility, maintenance, protection, and beautification of His creation. As we continue to examine what Scripture says about managing money and resources, this concept of stewardship will serve as a foundation.

Chapter Two

Reasons for Poverty

When considering the theme of stewardship from a biblical perspective, one of the first things we must look at is the biblical view of wealth and poverty. The Bible has much to say about these conditions. Some myths have been spread about what the Bible says in these areas; for example, one of the most misquoted verses in all of Scripture is this: "Money is the root of all evil." But the Bible doesn't say that. The King James Version says, "The love of money is the root of all evil" (1 Tim. 6:10; the modern

English Standard Version says, "The love of money is a root of all kinds of evils"). Wrongful motives for securing wealth can be dangerous; greed, theft, and other evils flow from such motives. The Bible warns us about pursuing wealth for its own sake, for "you cannot serve God and money" (Matt. 6:24). While money itself is neutral, our attitude toward it can be good or evil.

Because the Bible gives many warnings against the dangers of riches, some other misunderstandings have been perpetuated in the Christian community. One is that being wealthy is inherently sinful, or that only sinful people become wealthy. That's true in the sense that all people are sinful, but we find examples in the Scriptures of people who were fabulously wealthy, yet at the same time were virtuous and faithful. Abraham, for example, was the father of the faithful and also enormously wealthy. Likewise, Job was both godly and wealthy. Yet, Jesus also warns that it's hard for those who have riches to enter into the kingdom of God (Luke 18:25), principally because people who have an abundance of wealth can tend toward self-sufficiency and thus fail to rely upon God and His providence for meeting their daily needs.

Another myth that comes from this misunderstanding

is that there's some kind of inherent righteousness connected with being poor. In the Middle Ages, a movement developed within the church called "poverty mysticism," which associated such a degree of righteousness with poverty that people began to believe that through poverty one could enter into the kingdom of God. In our day, other myths abound. Some say that anyone who is poor is therefore blessed by God and is righteous; others claim that anyone who is poor is poor because they're lazy and refuse to work, and their poverty is then seen as a vice rather than a virtue. Both of these approaches to poverty and wealth are simplistic and don't really grapple with the biblical material concerning this issue. But all of them raise a broader question: Who are "the poor" in the Bible (see Luke 6:20)?

In a study of "the poor" in the Scriptures (both in the Old and New Testaments), a couple of things emerge immediately. The first is that poverty is always determined against some kind of standard. When it is said that someone is "poor," we have to ask, "Poor compared to what?" People in the United States today who subsist at what the U.S. government determines as the poverty level enjoy certain luxuries that even kings didn't enjoy just a few hundred years ago—electric light bulbs instead of candles, for instance. So, the whole notion of poverty and wealth is on a sliding scale. But apart from that—and more significantly—when we look at the Scriptures and consider this class of people who were called "the poor," we see that God is very concerned about these people. That concern differs, however, according to the distinctive characteristics of the various types of poor people that are described. We find in Scripture four distinct groups of people who are described as "poor," and we can see that God's response to these people is inseparably related to the reasons that they are poor.

The first group includes those who are poor as a result of some kind of calamity. The second is the person who is poor as a result of being oppressed or exploited. The third group of the poor in Scripture includes those who are poor due to sloth. And the fourth group describes those who, we would say, are poor for righteousness' sake. Let's look at these one by one.

The first group would include widows, widowers, and orphans, those who have lost a spouse or parent and therefore don't have a breadwinner to provide for them. If there is any group that is singled out for the special concern of the ministry of the Christian church, it is this category of poor people. James tells us, "Religion that is pure and undefiled before God, the Father, is this: to visit orphans and widows in their affliction, and to keep oneself unstained from the world" (James 1:27). Deacons were established in the early church with a specific charge of caring for the poor, especially for orphans and widows (Acts 6:1–7). The priority that was given to such people in biblical days has been somewhat lost today; we depend on the government and other agencies to take care of them rather than the church. But the church through the ages always has been called to be a ministering agent to those who are poor as a result of calamity.

This group includes not only widows, widowers, and orphans, but also those who have been incapacitated by illness, disease, or by an accident—for example, people who are left blind or lame and thus unable to be productive in the workplace. These people are singled out for specific care by the church in Scripture. It is the mandate of God for the church to go out of its way to support these people. The Old Testament laws regarding gleaning, for example, are a provision that God instituted to care for the needy who were unable to work for wages (see Deut. 24:19).

The second group of the poor found in the Old Testament consists of those who are reduced to poverty because of oppression or exploitation. We see this principally in the case of slavery. The people of Israel, when they were in bondage to the Egyptians, were impoverished because they were enslaved by a powerful government that used them as a slave labor force. This raises a question about another myth in our own culture: that the only way a person can ever become wealthy is at the expense of the poor. That may be true in a game where one person wins while another person loses. But there are many occupations and industries in which someone becomes wealthy in a way that works to the advantage of the poor, rather than at the expense of the poor.

An example is when Henry Ford introduced the concept of automation in the production of automobiles. Overnight, the price of a car was radically reduced because he had found a way to manufacture automobiles at a much lower cost than had been possible in the past. By mass-producing cars and increasing the number of units produced, he could lower the cost per unit. The result was that the automobile was brought within the reach of literally millions of people who previously had been unable to afford one. In the process, Henry Ford became fabulously wealthy. There are other examples of people who, through just and honest means, became wealthy without impoverishing other people.

But in the Old Testament era in particular, people often became poor through exploitation by government. Often, the wealthy people whom we read about in the Old Testament were governors who had amassed wealth through exploiting the people. Those who had the ability to exploit people for money were either those who had political power—governors, tyrants, kings, and so on—or criminals, who steal from and harm others in order to enrich themselves. Such people who become wealthy by exploiting others exist today as well, but not all people who become wealthy are criminals or people in government who exploit others.

The third group is one that's frequently addressed in the Old Testament, particularly in the book of Proverbs: those who are poor because of slothfulness. It is incorrect to say that every person who is poor is poor because he is lazy. However, it would be equally inaccurate to say that no one is poor because of slothfulness. The Old Testament describes a work ethic established in the garden of Eden and carried throughout the rest of Scripture. Some of the New Testament's statements regarding this work ethic are almost totally ignored in our culture, or they are addressed with outrage. Paul, for example, in writing to the church at Thessalonica, spoke about a certain group of people who would not work. They were idle and lazy, and they wanted to live off the contributions of other people. Paul gave this mandate to the church: "If anyone is not willing to work, let him not eat" (2 Thess. 3:10). That seems harsh and severe by contemporary standards, but Paul was simply reiterating the Old Testament work ethic that a person is responsible, if he is physically capable, for providing for himself and for his household, rather than looking to the community or the government to provide for his needs.

The book of Proverbs is replete with references to the slothful poor: "Go to the ant, O sluggard" (Prov. 6:6) and "As a door turns on its hinges, so does a sluggard on his bed" (Prov. 26:14). By contrast, Ecclesiastes tell us, "Sweet is the sleep of a laborer" (Eccl. 5:12). The hard-working man can put his head on the pillow at the end of a hard day's work knowing that he has been industrious and productive during that day, whereas for the lazy person, sleep is disturbed. The judgment of God is upon those who are poor because of slothfulness.

The fourth category of the poor are those who are poor

for righteousness' sake. They have made a conscious decision to forgo the acquisition of material wealth and riches for the sake of the kingdom of God and for the sake of serving others. These are people who have entered into ministry situations, who have skills that otherwise would make them capable of earning a better livelihood, but nevertheless are willing to forgo more lucrative enterprises for the sake of service. The supreme example of this kind of poverty is Christ Himself, who had no place to lay His head, who was willing to abandon His reputation and everything else for the sake of serving others. When the Bible describes this group of poor people, we see that God is enormously pleased with them and promises to give an abundance of honor and ultimate wealth to those who invest their time and energy in the service of the King. They will receive a great reward in heaven.

In looking at these four groups, we see that it is very dangerous to lump them all together and simply speak of "the poor," because there are such great differences between them. There are the poor who, through no fault of their own, have been impoverished by calamity that requires the ministry of the church. There are those who have been oppressed and exploited, and God hears their cries and groans even as He did in the exodus, saying to Pharaoh, "Let my people go." Those who are poor by reason of sloth incur the wrath of God and the judgment that they should not eat. Finally, those who are poor for righteousness' sake are blessed in the kingdom of God.

Chapter Three

The Building
of Wealth

I once heard Richard DeVos, cofounder of Amway and one of the world's wealthiest men, give a lecture on the material well-being of humanity. He asked his Christian audience, "Do you care about the material welfare of human beings? Because God obviously does."

This is a truth that is easy for us to forget. We can so spiritualize the things of God that we miss, for example, that Jesus Himself spoke of giving food to the hungry, giving shelter to the homeless, clothing the naked, and visiting those who are sick or in prison. In the Old Testament, physical prosperity was integral to the promises that God made to His people, which included "a land flowing with milk and honey" (Ex. 3:8). Not only that, but the ultimate fullness of redemption includes the promise of the resurrection of the body. We are not bound by Greek thought or dualistic categories that demean and denigrate the material world. We have been made as physical creatures with physical needs and desires. God, in His plan of redemption, is very concerned about that. Christians, as well, are bidden to be concerned about the material welfare of human beings, about people who are starving or ill, about those who are naked or homeless. These concerns are central to the Christian faith.

When speaking about material welfare, it is important to understand the conditions that bring it about. To do that, we must distinguish between *necessary* conditions and *sufficient* conditions. A necessary condition is something that must be true for another particular statement to be true. However, the truthfulness of the necessary condition does not guarantee that the consequent statement will be true. That would be a sufficient condition. Here's a classic example: Being a man is a necessary condition for John to be a bachelor, because a bachelor is an unmarried man. But John's being a man does not guarantee that he is a bachelor, because it's possible that he is married. Conversely, John's being a bachelor is a sufficient condition for his being a man, because a bachelor must be a man. With that in mind, we must understand what conditions are necessary for material welfare. While these conditions do not guarantee material welfare, they must exist for it to be possible.

In considering the causes for material well-being, the first necessary condition, and arguably the most important, is production. If we are concerned that people don't have any food, the most important thing to do is to produce food. If people are naked, our concern is not going to do any good unless we make clothes. Production must increase in order to alleviate poverty in physical areas.

As more goods are produced, the cost per unit drops. This is the law of supply and demand. If, for example, someone lives in a culture where the cost of making a shirt is almost prohibitive and a shirt is very expensive, only the wealthy can afford to own a shirt. But if production is increased so that each individual shirt becomes less expensive in the marketplace, then more people can avail themselves of shirts. The same is true with food. Farmers aren't always happy when there's a bumper crop because it drives the cost per unit down, but it also means that more people have the opportunity to buy food. So the single most important element for meeting the physical needs of human beings is the production of goods and services.

We must then explore what is necessary for increasing production. Some say it is more people in the workforce, while others say it is more industrious action by the producer. These are important, but the most important ingredient for rapidly increasing production is the use of tools. Look at it this way: I have a yard at home that needs to be mowed, and I have limited resources, three of which are time, energy, and money. How am I going to allocate these resources to cut my grass? The cheapest way that I could cut the grass is by getting on my hands and knees and biting off each blade of grass with my teeth. Doing it that way would expend a lot of time and energy, but not very much money. I could improve my production by getting a pair of scissors, and I could do it in less than half the time—but now there's some expense involved for the pair of scissors. I could get a push mower, which would increase my productivity enormously over a pair of scissors, but that is still more expensive. We could go from there to the power mower, from the power mower to the riding mower, and so on. With each step up, we do the job more quickly, and often better, though at an increasing cost. This principle applies in all other areas. We can produce more in less time than our forefathers could, not because we are smarter or stronger than they were, but because we have tools at our disposal that they didn't have.

The third necessary condition gets at why some people have tools and others don't. It is money. To buy tools, one has to have the money, or capital, to do it. More specifically, one must have surplus capital, which is capital that is left over after one has met one's obligations and paid one's expenses. Purchasing, maintaining, and updating equipment requires money in the form of surplus capital.

After World War II, the United States automobile industry ruled the world. By the 1970s, however, foreign automobile manufacturers began to compete heavily in the United States, and by the 1980s, Japanese car manufacturers were beating American manufacturers at their own game. Japan has few of the natural resources necessary for producing steel and building automobiles, while the United States has an abundance of such resources. Japanese manufacturers have to import their steel and other resources to build their cars, and then they have to pay to ship them across the Pacific Ocean—and they were still beating the American carmakers. One of the key things that happened with our chief competitors in the auto industry, Germany and Japan, was that their factories were virtually destroyed in World War II. Afterward, they had to build new factories with new equipment in order to be competitive in the second half of the twentieth century, whereas American plants were pouring their profits into marketing rather than into research and development or upgrading their factories. Suddenly, the American manufacturers had a product that was not competitive because they fell behind when it came to tools and production techniques.

The thing that drives the purchase and use of tools—which in turn increases production, which in turn gives the capacity to alleviate the problems of the poor and the needy—is profit. This is a point that every Christian needs to understand, because many have a negative view of profit. It has come to be seen as something obscene, as if there's something wrong when companies or individuals achieve profit or surplus capital. But without profit, there's no surplus, and without surplus, there's no investment in tools. Without the investment in tools, there can be no increase in production, which means the world remains hungry. Somewhere, somehow, someone has to be making a profit for there to be surplus capital in order to meet the needs of people in this world.

It's interesting how often Jesus used language borrowed from the marketplace and economics to communicate the spiritual truths of the gospel. One of the words that He uses frequently is *profit*. He said, "For what does it profit a man to gain the whole world and forfeit his soul?" (Mark 8:36; cf. Matt. 16:26; Luke 9:25). Jesus was saying that a person may have a material profit but the bottom line is in red ink—it is a loss—because he's exchanged something that is more valuable for something that is less valuable. We have to be careful about how we understand profit, being sure to look at it from the vantage point of the Scriptures.

God is intensely concerned about productivity. Even a cursory reading of the New Testament reveals constant references to the bearing of fruit, not just in the spiritual realm of discipleship, but in being productive, increasing one's talents and supply, and meeting more of the needs of people.

Chapter Four

The Theory
of Value

At a banquet I attended some years ago, one of the speakers was a former football player who played safety in the NFL. At one point in his career, he was earning $65,000 a year as a starter for his team. He recalled how his team played the Buffalo Bills during the prime of the infamous O.J. Simpson. On one play, O.J. broke loose at the line of scrimmage and made an eighty-five-yard touchdown run, breaking several tackles along the way—the last by the fellow who was giving the speech. As he came off the field afterward, his coach met him halfway, livid and red-faced, and screamed at him, "I'm paying you $65,000 a year to make that tackle." And the player said to the coach, "Yes, Coach, but Buffalo is paying O.J. $800,000 a year to break that tackle."

Debates over profits arise all the time, not just in regard to Wall Street but also regarding the sports world. Fans and non-fans alike heatedly debate the propriety of the profits that team owners receive and the large salaries that many players earn. In 1988, Orel Hershiser was the MVP of Major League Baseball's World Series. At the end of the season, he met with the team owner, Peter O'Malley, who gave him a contract that up to that point was the richest ever given to a baseball player. Hershiser is a devout Christian, and when the media announced to the world that he had signed this multimillion-dollar contract, he received an avalanche of letters protesting against his greed, accusing him of un-Christian concern for making so much money. The bulk of these letters came from people within the Christian community.

A mutual friend called and asked me if I would be willing to meet with Hershiser to discuss with him the ethics involved in his signing this lucrative baseball contract. I agreed, and I met with Orel at Vero Beach, Fla., during spring training. It was clear that he wanted to do the right thing; he asked me if he had sinned by signing a contract of this magnitude for his services. I replied, "I only have one question in terms of your stewardship and about the salary that you are receiving from the Los Angeles Dodgers: How much did your agent leave on the table in the negotiation?" His eyes became wide, and he said, "What do you mean?"

I said: "The minute your agent asked Peter O'Malley for one dollar more than he believed you were worth to his organization, Mr. O'Malley would say no. For that matter, if what Mr. O'Malley decided to pay you was one dollar less than what he was actually willing to pay you, he got you at bargain rates."

Orel laughed. No one else thought about it in terms of a bargain. But in the economics of that particular world of business, there was a free negotiation between the two people—a person who was offering his services and an owner who was offering a salary. The owner had to make the decision as to how much this performer was worth to his enterprise, and the player had to decide if he was willing to work for what the owner offered. That's what's going on all the time as these sports franchises increase in their value to the owners.

There's a lot of mythology surrounding profit in our culture. Imagine this scenario, which illustrates the concept of profit: A man owns a shoe store and buys a lot of shoes, and these shoes average out to thirty dollars a pair at the factory rate. He sets the price at ninety dollars on these shoes, and I purchase them for ninety dollars. Who makes the profit? First of all, the store owner makes a profit because he paid thirty dollars and sold them for ninety dollars. He bought low and sold high, making a profit of sixty dollars. Second, the manufacturer makes a profit because it doesn't cost him thirty dollars to make the pair of shoes.

But who else profits? The other person who profits in this transaction is the customer. Remember, there's no coercion involved; it's a free transaction. Every time someone goes shopping, they make choices. They choose which stores to enter, which goods to look at, and what price they are willing to pay for the things they want to buy. If the price of goods is more than they are willing to pay, they walk out—and, likewise, when the price is less than they are willing to pay, they buy, because they get what they want and still have money left over. This is another example of profit.

What makes this complicated—and the last example of profit more difficult to recognize—is the fact that this whole transaction involves money, a medium of exchange, rather than direct barter. Let's reimagine it as bartering instead. Suppose one man makes shoes and another man raises beef cows. The second man has a refrigerator filled with more steaks than he'll be able to eat in a lifetime, but he has a problem: his feet are cold, because he doesn't have any shoes. Next door there's the cobbler, who has a hundred pairs of shoes in his closet and so his feet are perfectly warm and dry. But what's his problem? He's hungry, because he doesn't have any meat to eat. So these two men strike a deal that will involve an exchange of goods at an agreed-upon rate that suits both parties. The cobbler says, "I'll trade you a pair of shoes for so many steaks," and the cattleman says, "Those shoes are more valuable to me than the surplus steaks that I have," so he makes the deal. That's bartering.

In that scenario, who profits? Both parties do. It's very clear that both sides profit in bartering. Thomas Aquinas said this was the way God ordained the whole universe to function in terms of meeting people's needs. No one really is self-sufficient; we live in a world community where we are interdependent. Our interdependence is the result of division of labor. We see this as early as the first family of mankind: with Cain and Abel, one was a farmer, the other a herder. They couldn't do both, so they would have exchanged goods and services. People have various gifts and skills that they bring to the universe of needs—some people bring rocket science, others bring accounting, and still others bring artistic gifts. We all need each other to live in this global village.

Initially, survival depended upon bartering. It was only after a new element was introduced, a substitute for exchange called currency or money, that people lost sight of the direct benefit that is involved in a free exchange of goods and services. When we see a simple barter transaction, it's clear how both sides profit. If we see a more contemporary exchange, where currency (which has no intrinsic value) is used instead, it is easy to lose sight of the mutual profitability of a free exchange. But everyone gains in a fair trade. That's what makes production work.

The other integral element of the business of profit in free trade is what economists call the "subjective theory of value." *Value* has to do with the worth that we ascribe to something. A good illustration of this is when someone wants to sell a car or trade it in at a dealership.

I once went to a dealership and spent a couple of hours

negotiating the price of a car with a salesman. I was finding it difficult to get him to tell me how much he would give me for my trade-in. Finally, he told me what he would give me for my car, and it was considerably less than I thought it would be. I said, "Well, I can't do the deal at that price," and he protested, "What I've just offered you is the actual value of your car." I said, "It may be the actual value of my car to you, but it is not the actual value of my car to me— because I would rather keep my car than give it to you in exchange for the amount you've offered me." Then I went down the street and found another dealer who set a higher value for my car and who was willing to give me more in exchange for it than the first dealer.

The point is, there is no such thing as an objective value for goods and services. It is all dependent on what we already have: things that are common, things that are scarce, and so on. That changes from person to person; we don't all have the same needs or wants, so we don't put the same value on everything.

The opposite of the subjective theory of value is a Marxist theory, called the "labor theory of value," which says that the price of a product should be determined by how much effort is involved by the worker in producing the product. The value, then, is established not by scarcity, market conditions, or by what people want or don't want, but simply by the effort that's involved.

To see the fallacy of that, just think of the difference in value between a painting by Lucas Cranach the Elder and a painting by R.C. Sproul. Cranach painted a famous portrait of Martin Luther that is worth millions of dollars. I have copied this painting myself. Suppose we went to an auction and put my painting next to Cranach's. Which painting do you think would be likely to receive the highest bid from the audience? There'd be no contest. I couldn't sell mine for a hundred dollars, whereas Cranach's is worth millions. The thing is, I'm sure it took me longer to paint my painting of Luther than it took Cranach to paint his. I had to work harder than he did. Why? Because he was much more skilled than I am. It's not how much effort I put into the product that makes it valuable; it's how other people value the product that determines its value for them.

We must always remember that prices are ultimately established by consumers. We determine the price of shoes, suits, tickets to basketball games, and everything else—because when the owner places his price above what consumers are willing to pay, they don't buy, and the owner's income drops. The only way he can profit is by offering his goods or services at a price that consumers regard as a profit to them when they make the purchase.

The basic theme of stewardship is that we are responsible before God for how we use the goods, services, and resources that are at our disposal. That means that a Christian steward is to be careful not to be wasteful with them. We need to measure the value of things we buy.

We make value judgments all the time, because every dollar we spend in one place is a dollar we can't spend somewhere else. So, though values are subjective in terms of our personal preferences, God has an ultimate value system of things that are much more weighty and much more important from the eternal perspective—and we must finally determine our values in light of His.

Chapter Five

What
Is Money?

The classical definition of money is "a medium of exchange." The term *medium* here refers to something that stands between two or more parties—a mode or an intermediate position through which things take place and interact. A medium of exchange refers to some means used to mediate the exchange of goods and services. This is instead of bartering, which is a direct exchange. In other words, money is an indirect form of exchange.

Money developed naturally and gradually over thousands

of years of bartering and trade as people looked for something that would simplify the whole process. It's one thing for us to look at the example of bartering that deals with similarly valued goods or services, such as when a shoemaker trades shoes for meat from the cattleman. But what does the shoemaker do when he wants to exchange shoes for a house? It's very difficult to calculate the cost of a whole house in terms of shoes, which makes it more challenging to have a fair exchange—all the more so when you consider that building a house involves a diversity of labor, with contributions from bricklayers, carpenters, roofers, electricians, and so on. How would we barter all of that in a practical way?

Currency emerged out of the need to simplify the exchange of goods and services. There had to be something that had value to everyone and that could be transported and divided with ease. Cultures throughout history have used various things as currency. Seashells were used in some civilizations. Native Americans used colored beads, because everyone had a use for beads in their clothing. In the American Colonies, tobacco became the currency for a while. But beads can be easily lost or broken, and tobacco can rot. So, imperishability also became an important criterion for a stable currency. Eventually, two substances emerged in the dynamics of the marketplace as the preferred medium of exchange: gold and silver. They had stability, utility, and just enough scarcity to maintain a stable value over time.

When Joseph was sold into slavery in Genesis 37:28, he was sold for twenty pieces of silver. Already by that time in the Mediterranean basin, silver was used as a medium of exchange, and we know that gold was also. The Bible talks elsewhere about the minting of coins, as when Jesus refers to a picture and inscription on a coin (Matt. 22:17–21; cf. Mark 12:14–17; Luke 20:22–25). There is a long history and tradition of the use of gold and silver for currency so that people would not have to engage in direct barter or trade. Instead of exchanging steaks for shoes, one could exchange gold for shoes or gold for steaks.

Once this system emerged of using silver and gold, the next phase in the development of currency was the development of what might be called gold and silver warehouses. People didn't always have safe places to keep their silver and gold, so someone would operate a warehouse where others could, for a fee, deposit their gold and silver for safekeeping. Whenever people deposited gold and silver in the warehouse, they received a receipt for the amount they had on deposit. Later, money became even more sophisticated when, instead of directly exchanging the gold or silver for goods or services, people simply began to exchange their receipts. This was the development of checks, where a piece of paper that has no intrinsic value becomes valuable because it is a marker or a receipt that entitles someone else to cash it in for real currency that is stored in the warehouse. That's how we eventually arrived at paper currency. Paper currency is a kind of check, although it used to be a more direct form of it. Paper bills in the United States used to be "gold certificates" or "silver certificates," which meant they entitled the bearer to some amount of gold or silver.

Over time, our economic system has moved away from gold and silver as the standard for currency. Now we have checks or paper receipts without any intrinsic value and without any gold or silver to back them up, but which have been established as currency by law. Such currency is known as "fiat" money, from the Latin meaning "let it be." The government grants such currency the status of "legal tender," meaning that under ordinary circumstances it must be accepted as payment. This means that if someone goes into a store that sells televisions for three hundred dollars and offers three hundred pieces of paper marked "legal tender"—not silver or gold certificates—then the person selling the television is bound by law to accept those pieces of paper as payment in full for the goods that he is selling. There are a couple of things that back up fiat money: first, the authority of the government. The government says you must accept it as a medium of exchange for goods and services even though there's nothing of real value behind it. That puts legal force behind it. Second, there is public confidence that the government is not going to allow the system to fall apart.

But there are two problems that emerge immediately: first, the confidence placed in currency is limited to the borders of the government that gives it authority. The second problem that emerges is that, historically, governments tend to default. People engage in enormous risk when they exchange goods and services on the basis of paper that has nothing to back it up. As long as everyone trusts it, it continues to work—but it's a dangerous business, and, incidentally, one that has a clear biblical prohibition. God instituted in the nation of Israel a law against the debasing of currency. In the ancient world, where gold and silver were used as a medium of exchange, sometimes unscrupulous people would "clip" a coin; they would clip off a tiny piece of gold from a gold coin and keep it for themselves. The result was that a coin of a certain face value, say, one hundred dollars, no longer contained one hundred dollars' worth of gold. This was seen by God as a serious sin because it defrauded people in the enterprise of exchanging goods and services. So the biblical law against the debasement of currency is extremely clear and strong.

There is another law from economics called Gresham's Law, which says simply, "Bad money drives out good." I once did an experiment with seventh- and eighth-graders to teach this principle. A student had a five-dollar bill, and I asked if I could make a deal with him to buy his money. I offered him a nickel, then a dime, and then a quarter. Then I offered him seventy-five cents—a quarter and fifty-cent piece together. Then I offered him a dollar, and finally five dollars. He turned all of these deals down, because he couldn't see any advantage to selling his five-dollar bill to me for any of the offers that I made. I asked everyone in the class, "Was he a good businessman?" and they all agreed that he was. I said, "No, he wasn't," and I called attention to when I had offered him a quarter and a fifty-cent piece. I revealed that the fifty-cent coin I'd offered him was a 1939 Liberty half-dollar, the silver value of which is far greater than its face value (I had purchased it for forty dollars). He didn't recognize it; he'd never seen a half-dollar like this because it had been out of circulation for so long. The reason why it's out of circulation is Gresham's Law.

To understand Gresham's law, we must understand what bad money and good money are. Bad money is coinage that has been alloyed with another substance, making it less valuable, or paper money that has nothing backing it. Good money is hard currency that has intrinsic value, as silver and gold do. Bad money drives good money out of circulation for the simple reason that people tend to value hard currency above its face value. People would see it as wasteful to spend a Liberty fifty-cent piece for a fifty-cent item in the marketplace. So, given the choice, people would rather spend currency with less or no intrinsic value and hold on to their hard currency. This tends to push hard currency out of circulation.

These are just some of the elementary principles of money, but they are things that we need to understand. Money, in terms of its current currency value, has almost no intrinsic value. How is it possible that we, as a nation, will exchange beautiful paintings, homes, clothing, food, televisions, or automobiles for paper? Because we haven't really understood that there's no intrinsic value in the paper—and as long as everybody's doing it, it tends to work. But the lessons of history also indicate that currency that is not backed up by something of real value eventually collapses, and the wise steward takes non-valuable paper and converts it as quickly and as wisely as he can into items of real value.

Chapter Six

Inflation

On election day in 1992, one of the questions asked of voters by pollsters was, "Are you concerned about inflation?" That particular poll found that 5 percent of Americans who voted in the 1992 U.S. presidential election were concerned about inflation. That is a remarkable statistic, because only a few elections earlier, at the end of the administration of President Jimmy Carter, it was the central issue of the presidential election. During Carter's administration, inflation rose to double-digit rates, which caused a panic and even a crisis in our whole economic system. President Carter made the observation that inflation was the cruelest tax of all, because it hits the poor and the elderly the hardest.

When I ask students what inflation is, the answer I frequently hear is that it is a rise in prices for goods and services. But that is not quite accurate. A rise in prices is not inflation, but the result of it. Inflation itself is simpler than that; technically, it is an increase in money supply. When there is more money in circulation, it has an impact upon prices and people. In this chapter, we'll use a simplified example to try to gain a better understanding of what that impact is.

Imagine a fictional town, where the economy is based upon a hundred dollars' worth of money that is in circulation. Everything in the village is priced according to the amount of money that is in circulation. Suppose I live in this town, and I have a problem: I have borrowed money from the bank, and I owe the bank ten dollars. The problem is, I can't pay what I owe. So I come up with a scheme. I carefully design a counterfeit ten-dollar bill, and I use that to pay off my debt. The bank doesn't realize that I paid them in fake money, and now counterfeit money has been added to the village's money supply.

By creating a counterfeit ten-dollar bill, I have increased the supply of money in circulation from $100 to $110, or by 10 percent. What does that do to the value of the money that was already there? It now declines by 10 percent. More money in the money supply means less value per unit of currency. Because it is less valuable, it also has less purchasing power.

Who benefits in this situation? The first person who benefits is the one who printed the counterfeit ten dollars because he paid off his debt. The second one that benefits is the bank, because it had its money repaid and it was then able to continue performing transactions. And anyone who owed money to someone else at a fixed rate also benefits. If someone had borrowed a dollar from the bank, the dollar that they pay back is worth the equivalent of ninety cents at the time they borrowed it.

That's why, in America in the 1960s, one of the best investments a person could make was the purchase of a house. Inflation was rising at such a pace that people could pay off their loans with less-valuable currency than what they had borrowed initially. That's still happening, though not at the same rate. However, if the inflation rate hovers around 4 percent for twenty-five years, someone would pay back a loan that they borrowed twenty-five years earlier with money that's worth half as much as when they borrowed it. And yet, a 4 percent inflation rate doesn't seem to be a big deal.

So debtors benefit from the increase in the money supply, but who gets hurt? First of all, the poor and the elderly do, because they tend to be on fixed incomes. They are not getting cost-of-living increases in their retirement payments or pay rates. If inflation this year is 4 percent, then next year people who are living on fixed incomes will have 96 percent of the purchasing power that they had this year. And each year that they stay alive, they lose more wealth and have a greater problem.

Why was it such a problem that only 5 percent of the people in America were concerned about inflation in the 1992 election? Because one big economic issue is the problem of the U.S. government's budget deficit, which, by the late 1980s, had risen to more than $200 billion a year. Suppose I open a lemonade stand and want to make it into a profitable enterprise. I sell my glasses of lemonade for five cents—but then I figure out that it costs me ten cents per glass to make and sell the lemonade. Can I make up that deficit in volume? No—the more lemonade I sell, the worse off I become. If I am running my little lemonade stand at a loss, sooner or later I'll have to make adjustments, or I'm out of business. When a government constantly operates at a deficit and that deficit is growing exponentially, it means it is spending more money than it is taking in.

There are three basic things that can be done to address the deficit problem. The first is to cut costs. This is what happens when downsizing takes place in businesses. What happens if the government sets out to cut $200 billion worth of expenses? A lot of people will be unemployed. Programs that people have become accustomed to receiving will be cut. This—cutting programs especially—is one of the most unpopular things that a government can do. So, that's a tenuous means of solving the problem.

The second option is to increase revenue. There aren't many things that the government does to get revenue, but the number one way that governments increase their revenue is by raising taxes. But tax rates are already higher than people would like, so that's also an extremely unpopular method of increasing financial stability.

The third option is to increase the money supply, because the government is the debtor. The government can increase the money supply at will, which makes it the only organization that has the legal right to do what essentially amounts to counterfeiting. It can, if it so chooses, produce as much money as it wants. History has shown that when governments are deeply in debt, they start up the printing presses in earnest.

How does inflation affect your family, your life, and the goods and the services that you need for medical care, clothing, food, and housing? The first home I purchased cost me twenty-one thousand dollars. Some years later, that same house, which was then considerably older, sold for more than two hundred thousand dollars. I've been to countries where people will spend one hundred thousand units of the local currency for a loaf of bread. When the currency was first established in that nation, do you suppose that anyone would have sought to create a system that would demand one hundred thousand of anything for a loaf of bread? That happens when governments debase currency over and over again, so that it requires one hundred thousand or one million units of currency to purchase what used to cost one thousand units. When this happens, people lose the basic resources that they've worked their whole lives to accumulate.

Chapter Seven

Interest

When we look at the biblical mandate for Christian stewardship, one of the most important things to consider is how we allocate the resources that God has given to us. There are lots of things that we can consider resources—the abilities that we have, our homes and other property, the air that we breathe, and so on. But our basic resources include our time, our labor, our talents, and our money. At one point at least, we all are on a level playing field, and that's with respect to the allocation of time. Each one of us has the same number of hours in every day. The busiest man in the world has twenty-four hours in a day, and the laziest man in the world has the same twenty-four hours. The New Testament is very concerned with how we use our time. The Apostle Paul, for example, tells us that we are to make the best use of our time, because "the days are evil" (Eph. 5:16). This means we must use our time wisely, in a manner that is productive for the welfare of people and for the cause of the kingdom of God.

When it comes to the allocation of resources such as time, discipline is required, and also wisdom. This is the case also with how we use our financial resources. Because a dollar that we spend in one place is a dollar that we cannot spend somewhere else, we must make wise decisions about how we're going to spend our money.

Perhaps one of our greatest problems is wasting money. Jesus addresses this issue in the parable of the talents (Matt. 25:14–30). Some people think He's talking about gifts or abilities, but really He meant money, because a *talent* was a unit of currency. Jesus talks about how one person wasted his money while the other one doubled it. How we use our resources—in this case, our money—is a matter of concern to God, because we are to be good stewards with what He has entrusted to us.

There are some basic principles of stewardship that Scripture gives us, not the least of which is a common-sense one: we are called, as responsible stewards of the kingdom of God and of whatever abundance God has been pleased to give to us, to live within our means. Not everyone makes the same amount of money, but we all have the responsibility to live according to whatever that amount happens to be. Unfortunately, our culture has a chronic tendency to live at a deficit. This is a problem for the government, but perhaps even more dangerously in our own households. Surveys say that more than half of Americans live beyond their means; that is, they spend more money than they take in. Most often, that's done through credit, borrowing and indebting oneself to others.

I once got a haircut from a woman who asked me if I'd ever won anything in the Florida lottery. I said no, I hadn't, and she asked me how often I play. I said, "Never. I have never purchased a lottery ticket." When she asked why not, I told her, "I can't afford it." She laughed at me; she thought I was joking. She told me how much money per week she spent on lottery tickets. I knew that she didn't make a lot of money in her profession, so while she was cutting my hair I got out my pocket calculator. Then I said to her, "If I gave you sixty thousand dollars today as a gift, would you like that?" She said yes. I said, "Well, would you take that sixty thousand dollars and spend it on lottery tickets?" She laughed and said, "Of course not." I said, "But that's what you're doing."

I showed her with my calculator, taking the amount of money that she spent in a year on lottery tickets, and calculating what would happen if she invested the same amount of money and was blessed enough to earn a 10 percent annual rate of interest on her savings over a period of twenty years. In that time, she would have amassed sixty thousand dollars. But she just couldn't conceive of how she could multiply this small amount of money to such a large amount in twenty years. So. I began to explain to her about compound interest, which is what Jesus was speaking about, indirectly at least, in the parable of the talents.

As I mentioned previously, I once taught a group of seventh- and eighth-graders on the principles of stewardship and economics. At one point, I asked them this question: "If, when you graduate from college and get your first real job, you invest one thousand dollars a year for twenty years, and you're blessed enough to earn a 10 percent annual return on that one thousand dollars, how much money would you have at the end of the twenty years?" First of all, they guessed; they said, "A thousand dollars each year for twenty years is twenty thousand dollars; 10 percent of twenty thousand is two thousand. So it must be twenty-two thousand dollars." I said, "But you haven't understood how interest compounds in this process." So I took them through what they would have after the first year with a 10 percent gain, and after the second year and the third year. Then I showed them that, after twenty years, instead of twenty-two thousand dollars, they would have about sixty-three thousand dollars. They were amazed.

Let's say that you're going to embark on an investment program where, in the first year, you invest one thousand dollars, and the second year you add five hundred dollars to your principal investments—so in the second year, you invest fifteen hundred dollars. Each year thereafter for twenty years, you increase the amount of money that you save or invest by five hundred dollars, so that the third year you would be investing two thousand and by the fourth year twenty-five hundred and so on. In the twentieth year, you would be investing $10,500. Now, suppose that you are able to earn 10 percent annually in return. After twenty years, you would have almost a quarter of a million dollars.

Some will ask, "How can I afford to be increasing my investment by that level each year? I don't have that kind of money to invest, and even the initial investment of a thousand dollars a year seems big." But take a person who is in his twenties and just entering his career. Suppose he starts his career earning fifty thousand dollars a year, and he also tithes. The first thing he does is pay two thousand dollars to God, and he also has to pay his taxes. At this point, all he needs to do is put 5 percent of his income toward investment. Most people like this will be in an upward growth pattern whereby their salaries increase year after year. After a period of twenty years at their job, if they're careful and wise in their handling of their resources, they are more able to afford a larger amount to invest.

The other big question people have is, "Where am I able to get 10 percent interest?" They won't get it in a savings account at a bank. But there are very good investment companies that will help small investors allocate their resources. I've done this for years, and I have never yet had a year that the return on my investments is lower than 10 percent.

Why don't more of us invest like this? The biggest

problem we have is the temptation for quick gratification. We want to enjoy the fruit of our labor now, whereas a tolerance for delayed gratification is necessary for this kind of investment. We must put off buying things that we want to buy and consume to a later time, because we are trying to be responsible as stewards with our investments.

But the other side of the problem is that compounding interest can work in both directions. Not only can it work for us, as we delay our gratification and invest, but it can work against us if we spend more than we make and begin to borrow money. We have to repay that money on a compounded basis. That's where many of us get into serious financial problems, because instead of earning interest on our money, we allow someone else to earn money from us when we pay interest. If more than half of Americans are living beyond their means, they are doing this; the law of compound interest is working against them.

I hardly ever carry much cash around with me. But I have to admit, I have a wallet full of credit cards. I love credit cards because I don't have to use cash. I can go into stores, pull out the plastic, charge whatever I want to buy, and then at the end of the month I get a bill and I pay it. That's the convenience of credit cards. But I'll tell you something else about my credit cards: my wife and I have never paid a single penny of interest on credit card purchases.

Credit cards issuers routinely charge 18 percent interest, and sometimes 26 percent or more, if you don't pay off the balance each month. That's why so many of us are in debt. It's so easy and tempting to purchase with plastic. Enjoy the goods now; worry about paying for them later. But if you can't pay for it at the end of month, now you have to carry a balance on which you will be charged interest. I can't afford to do that, and I don't think many of us can. If you're struggling with your finances, perhaps the best thing you could do today is take your credit cards and throw them in the trash. That way, you'll stop buying your way into debt.

Chapter Eight

Participating
in Ownership

As a boy, I lived near a steel mill town in Western Pennsylvania. I would often drive past the mill on a Friday afternoon, when the men would come off their shift, and I would watch them go to the paymaster's window to get their weekly paycheck. These were men who were engaged in really hard labor. I noticed that it was like a parade from the paymaster's office to the local bars. There were so many bars in the town that you almost couldn't count them, and the vast majority of the men, after working so hard for their wages, came out of the mill, went straight to the bar, and, in many cases, drank up their paycheck.

Another handful of these men came away from the paymaster's booth and went to one of two places: they either went to the bank, where they deposited their paycheck, or they went home and gave their paycheck to their wives. This group was determined to live within their means, even though it was not a high level of income. They saved their money because they were committed to it. They said: "I hate this job; it is so hard and so draining. I don't want my kids to have to work like I've had to work. I want them to get a college education." So, little by little, they deferred their own gratification for the sake of their children.

These men took seriously, whether they were believers or not, the biblical injunction to provide for one's household. By contrast, I've seen bumper stickers on the expensive cars of retired couples that say, "We're spending our children's inheritance." I don't think that's a funny joke. As a father and a husband, I have a moral obligation to try to live within my means, to spend less than I earn, so that I can give to my children and to my wife some substance that they can use in their needed provisions for their lifetime. The Apostle Paul said, "If anyone does not provide for his relatives, and especially for members of his household, he has denied the faith and is worse than an unbeliever" (1 Tim. 5:8). It is our duty as Christians to provide for our families, and that provision involves a wise use of whatever resources we have at our disposal.

I saw examples like those men at the steel factory so often in Pittsburgh because at that time it was the labor capital of America. I grew up in that city. My great-grandfather on my father's side came from Ireland. He immigrated to this country and settled in Pittsburgh in the nineteenth century. When he arrived at the shores of America, he was barefoot. He left behind a life of poverty during the potato famine in northern Ireland, where he lived in a cottage with a thatched roof and a mud floor. He arrived here virtually penniless. On the other hand, my great-grandfather on my mother's side was part of the landed aristocracy of Yugoslavia, and he also came to this country in the nineteenth century. One side of my family had its roots in comfortable financial affluence in the old country, whereas the patriarch on the other side was virtually a pauper.

Now, let me tell you about my grandparents. My grandfather on my father's side became a prominent businessman in Pittsburgh; by the time he died, he was the owner and president of the largest corporate bankruptcy firm in the city. My grandfather on my mother's side, the son of the landed aristocrat who migrated to this country, died in his thirties—penniless. The only job he ever had in this country was a job that involved unskilled labor. Why? The family fortunes reversed themselves in one generation for a simple reason: language. In nineteenth-century Pittsburgh, the chief industry was steel. Andrew Carnegie, the famous industrialist and philanthropist, dominated the industry. Carnegie was looking for people who spoke English to be managers, so many of those who came from English-speaking parts of the world rose to positions of management. On the other hand, those who came from Eastern Europe and other places where English was not spoken were unable to communicate, so they were left to perform unskilled labor. Just the language barrier made a huge difference from one generation to the next. That's something we can't always control, but how we use whatever we do have makes a difference.

The basic concept of capitalism is that we should let our money work for us rather than against us. Karl Marx understood some of that profoundly, although he developed a system that is quite different from capitalism. He understood the principle of economics that tools are crucial to increasing production. Marx said in effect: "Whoever owns the tools, rules the world. And everyone else has to work for the person who owns the tools." He concluded that there is fundamentally no difference between a wage earner and a slave, because the wage earner is always at the mercy of the person who owns the business or owns the tools. Therefore, the only just society is where the state owns the means of production. So, in Marx's system, the tools and means of production are taken out of the hands of private owners and put into the hands of the people as a whole, as embodied in the state. The problem, as history has demonstrated, is that when everyone owns everything, no one owns anything. Everyone gets an equal share of the pie, but the pie just keeps getting smaller and smaller.

Marx also understood that economic freedom comes from ownership. The people who own the big businesses are the ones who make economic fortunes—not, usually, the people who work for them. That's why the American dream has so often been the dream of ownership. There's good news about that, and then there's bad news.

Have you ever dreamed of owning your own business? Wouldn't it be great to be your own boss rather than working for someone else and being paid a salary while they're making a lot of money from your labor? The good news is that owning your own business means that you make the rules, you set your own hours, and you receive the profits of the business. You take pride in your business and in participating in the American dream. So, owning your own business can be a wonderful way to meet your goals in life and experience economic freedom.

The bad news is that owning your own business can be extremely difficult. I once read some statistics that said that every year in the United States, five hundred thousand new businesses begin, and at the end of the first year, four hundred thousand of those are still in existence. Twenty percent, or one hundred thousand, fail in the first year. At the end of five years, three hundred thousand more of those businesses will have failed and will no longer exist. After ten years, only twenty-thousand of those businesses will still exist. That's 4 percent. That means that 96 percent of businesses that start up in America fail in the first ten years.

The two greatest reasons for business failure are these: first, the business doesn't have enough capital to start with, and second, it is poorly managed, that is, the resources are not allocated properly. It goes like this: a shoemaker works in a shoe shop, but doesn't own the shoe shop. He's good at fixing shoes and he dreams of the day when he can open his own store. Because he has this craftsmanship, he saves his money, buys a little place, and opens up his own business—not realizing that to own and run the store requires financial knowledge, marketing knowledge, and all kinds of other things that he never counted on needing before he opened his business. He could very soon run into trouble. Yet the dream is there for ownership, because Marx was right: ownership can bring financial prosperity.

But there is another way besides owning your own business, and it's the way those steelworkers in Pittsburgh did it. When they went to the paymaster's window on Friday afternoon and got their paycheck, instead of drinking it away, some took a small percentage and bought stock in the steel company. It wasn't much, but they participated in owning the company. Every time they got a paycheck, they invested it in a business that was stable and secure. Then, when they went home from work and went to bed, the steel mill was still operating and they were still earning a reward for their labor, because their money was working for them.

So another basic principle of stewardship, which I believe is biblical because it has to do with prudence and wisdom, is this: As much as is humanly possible, make every expenditure an investment. How do you do that? Think back to the discussion about bartering. We saw that, in the system of trade and bartering, when the man traded his shoes for steaks, and the other man traded his steaks for shoes, both sides profited, and both sides were able to increase their material well-being—in other words, to increase their wealth.

For example, when someone buys groceries at the store, they spend money in exchange for goods and foodstuffs. They need those things. They buy tomatoes and oranges not so that they can sell them for a higher price on the street corner, but so they can eat. They are investing in their own life, in their physical future. They can waste their money on food by buying junk food, but it's not good for them. When it comes to things like cars, clothes, and furniture, it is smart to buy used, to buy things that will last, or to buy things that won't drop sharply in value. There are a lot of ways that we can purchase goods and services that will appreciate in value rather than depreciate. It's not just a matter of saving money by putting it in a bank or investing it, but being careful in the spending that we do.

In this book, we've looked at some basic principles of stewardship and economics. We've talked about investments, delayed gratification, and participating in ownership if even in a small way. But the most important investment we can ever make is in the kingdom of God. Tithing is not a net loss. I have never missed a single penny that I have given to the work of God. The older I get, the more I go beyond tithing, because I see the importance of investing in the best long-term investment there is. I'm not saying you should give your tithe so that God will open up the windows of heaven and give you a shower of blessing. I'm talking about investing in that which has eternal significance and eternal value.

About the Author

Dr. R.C. Sproul was founder of Ligonier Ministries, founding pastor of Saint Andrew's Chapel in Sanford, Fla., first president of Reformation Bible College, and executive editor of *Tabletalk* magazine. His radio program, *Renewing Your Mind,* is still broadcast daily on hundreds of radio stations around the world and can also be heard online. He was author of more than one hundred books, including *The Holiness of God, Chosen by God,* and *Everyone's a Theologian.* He was recognized throughout the world for his articulate defense of the inerrancy of Scripture and the need for God's people to stand with conviction upon His Word.

Free eBooks *by* R.C. Sproul

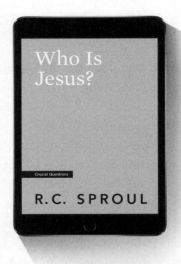

Get 3 free months of *Tabletalk*

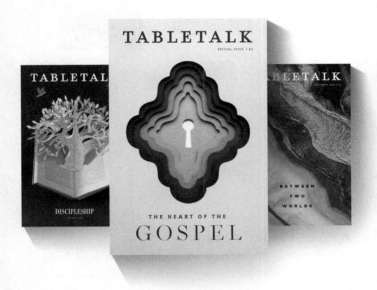

In 1977, R.C. Sproul started *Tabletalk* magazine.
Today it has become the most widely read subscriber-based monthly
devotional magazine in the world. **Try it free for 3 months.**

ASK LIGONIER

Do we have free will?

Is it true that God controls everything?

Why did God kill Uzzah?

A Place to Find Answers

Maybe you're leading a Bible study tomorrow. Maybe you're just beginning to dig deeper. It's good to know that you can always ask Ligonier. For more than forty-five years, Christians have been looking to Ligonier Ministries, the teaching fellowship of R.C. Sproul, for clear and helpful answers to biblical and theological questions. Now you can ask those questions as they arise, confident that our team will work quickly to provide clear, concise, and trustworthy answers. When you have questions, just ask Ligonier.